# THE WORLD'S GREATEST
# TANKS

## Ian Graham

**Raintree**

www.raintreepublishers.co.uk
Visit our website to find out more information about Raintree books.

To order:
 Phone 44 (0) 1865 888112
 Send a fax to 44 (0) 1865 314091
Visit the Raintree Bookshop at www.raintreepublishers.co.uk to browse our catalogue and order online.

First published in Great Britain by Raintree, Halley Court, Jordan Hill, Oxford, OX2 8EJ, part of Harcourt Education.
Raintree is a registered trademark of Harcourt Education Ltd.

© Harcourt Education Ltd 2006
First published in paperback in 2007
The moral right of the proprietor has been asserted.

Editorial: Andrew Farrow and Dan Nunn
Design: Ron Kamen and Philippa Baile
Picture Research: Hannah Taylor and Elaine Willis
Production: Victoria Fitzgerald

Originated by Dot Gradations Ltd.
Printed in China

The paper used to print this book comes from sustainable resources.

ISBN 13: 978 1844 212651 (HB)
ISBN 10: 1 844 21265 3 (HB)
10 09 08 07 06
10 9 8 7 6 5 4 3 2 1

ISBN 13: 978 1844 212842 (PB)
ISBN 10: 1 844 21284 X (PB)
10 09 08 07
10 9 8 7 6 5 4 3 2 1

**British Library Cataloguing in Publication Data**
Graham, Ian, 1953-
 Tanks. – (The world's greatest)
 1. Tanks (Military science) – Juvenile literature
 I. Title
 623.7'4752
A full catalogue record for this book is available from the British Library.

**Acknowledgements**
The publishers would like to thank the following for permission to reproduce photographs:

AKG pp. **8** (ullstein – Fotoagentur imo), **16** (ullstein – SV-Bilderdienst), **19** (ullstein – SV-Bilderdienst); Associated Press pp. **21**, **23**; Corbis pp. **9 top** (Reuters/Alexei Vladykin), **9 bottom** (Robin Adshead/The Military Picture Library), **13** (Bettmann), **22** (Reuters/Richard Chung); Corbis Sygma p. **10** (Gyori Antoine); General Dynamics Land Systems p. **25 bottom**; Getty Images pp. **4 left** (Hulton Archive), **4 right** (Time Life Pictures), **5**, **6** (Time Life Pictures), **11 bottom** (AFP), **18** (Hulton Archive), **20** (AFP), **24** (Time Life Pictures); Imperial War Museum p. **17**; Repaircraft PLC pp. **1**, **12**; Reuters p. **11 top** (Kim Kyung-Hoon); Swedish Defence Images pp. **14** (Lasse Siogren), **15** (Lasse Siogren); United States Department of Defence p. **25 top**.

Cover photograph of an M1-A2 Abrams tank reproduced with permission of Getty Images/ Time Life Pictures.

Every effort has been made to contact copyright holders of any material reproduced in this book. Any omissions will be rectified in subsequent printings if notice is given to the publishers.

# Contents

Words appearing in the text in bold, **like this**, are explained in the Glossary.

# Tanks

The tank is a powerful weapon of war. It has a big gun that can destroy other tanks and vehicles. The gun is in a **turret** that can turn and point in any direction.

## What are tanks for?

At first, soldiers used tanks to help them attack enemy soldiers. Tanks moved forward with soldiers sheltering behind them. When they reached the enemy, the soldiers did the fighting. Soon afterwards, tanks began to fight other tanks.

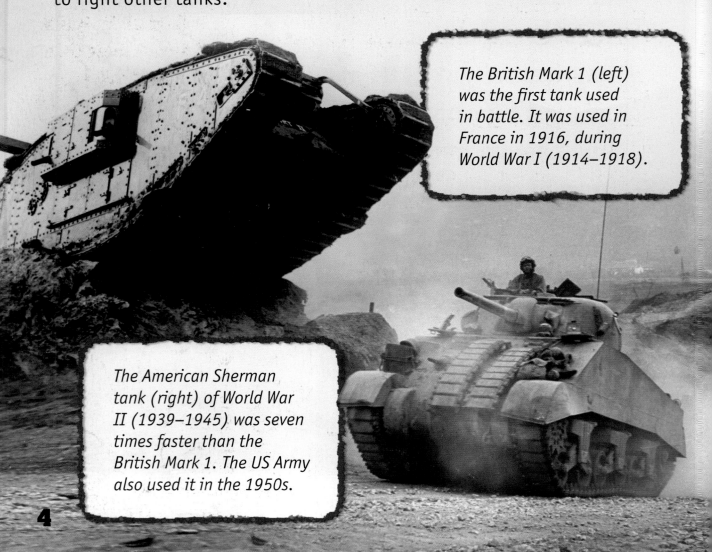

The British Mark 1 (left) was the first tank used in battle. It was used in France in 1916, during World War I (1914–1918).

The American Sherman tank (right) of World War II (1939–1945) was seven times faster than the British Mark 1. The US Army also used it in the 1950s.

> *Tanks can cover ground fast in desert warfare.*

## Taking the weight

Tanks have thick **armour** to protect the crew. Thick armour is heavy. Tanks would sink into soft ground if they had wheels like other vehicles. Instead, they have **tracks** – one on each side. Tracks spread a tank's weight evenly over the ground. This stops it sinking.

## Steering

A tank cannot turn its tracks to go round a bend. A tank turns by slowing down or stopping one of its tracks. It acts like a brake on that side of the tank. The other track keeps going and pushes the tank round.

### WORLD TANKS

There are more than 110,000 tanks used by armies all over the world.

|  | **Mark I** | **M4 Sherman** |
|---|---|---|
| *In service:* | World War I | World War II |
| *Crew:* | 8 | 5 |
| *Top speed:* | 6 kph/4 mph | 42 kph/26 mph |
| *Weight:* | 28,450 kg/62,720 lb | 31,555 kg/69,565 lb |
| *Armament:* | Two 6-pounder guns and four **machine-guns** | A 75-mm main gun, three machine-guns, and a 2-inch **mortar** |

# The world's best tank

The world's most advanced tank is the American M1 Abrams. It is designed to be able to destroy any other tank. The latest model is the M1A2. The M1A2 is nearly twice as heavy as a big road truck. It is almost three times as powerful.

## Inside the Abrams

The Abrams tank has a crew of four soldiers. The **commander** is in charge of the tank. He sits in the turret. The **gunner** sits in front of the commander. The gunner aims and fires the gun. The **loader** sits beside the commander. His job is to load the gun. The driver sits at the front of the tank.

*The Abrams tank is very low. This makes it hard to shoot at.*

## Jet power

Most tanks have **diesel engines**, like those used by road trucks. The Abrams tank has a **gas turbine engine**. It works like the jet engine of a fighter-plane. It is as powerful as ten car engines!

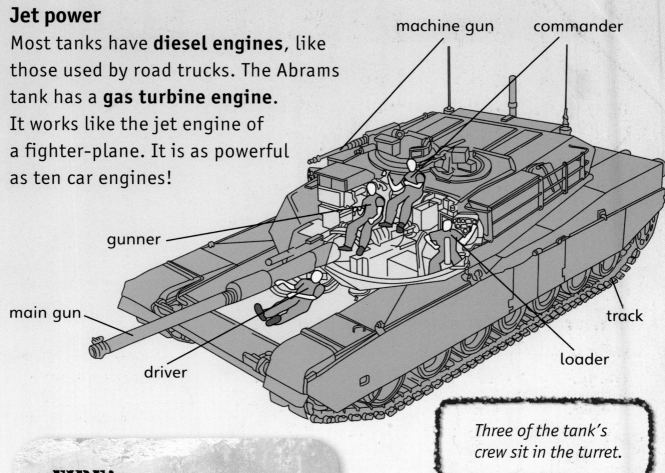

machine gun

commander

gunner

main gun

driver

track

loader

Three of the tank's crew sit in the turret.

## FIRE!

The Abrams tank uses a laser and computers to fire its **main gun** very accurately. It can hit targets four kilometres (more than two miles) away.

| | Abrams tank | Road truck |
|---|---|---|
| Crew: | 4 | 1 |
| Engine power: | 1,500 horse power | Up to 600 horsepower |
| Engine type: | Gas turbine | Diesel |
| Weight: | 70,655 kg/155,770 lb | Up to 36,285 kg/80,000 lb |
| Armament: | 120-mm main gun and 3 machine-guns | None |

# Other main battle tanks

Many other countries have **main battle tanks**. These include Germany's Leopard 2, Britain's Challenger 2, and the Russian T-90.

## Leopard tracks

The Leopard 2 has a diesel engine as powerful as the engine in the American Abrams tank. That makes it very fast for a battle tank. New Leopard 2 tanks have a gun with a longer **barrel**. It lets the Leopard 2 hit targets further away, up to 5,000 metres (3 miles).

*The Leopard 2's engine can be taken out for repair or replacement in only 15 minutes.*

| | Challenger 2 | Leopard 2 | T-90 |
|---|---|---|---|
| Crew: | 4 | 4 | 3 |
| Top speed: | 60 kph/37 mph | 72 kph/45 mph | 60 kph/37 mph |
| Weight: | 62,500 kg/137,790 lb | 62,000 kg/136,685 lb | 46,500 kg/102,515 lb |
| Armament: | 120-mm main gun and 2 machine-guns | 120-mm main gun and 2 machine-guns | 125-mm main gun and 2 machine-guns |

*The Russian T-90 tank has a smaller crew than most main battle tanks. It has a crew of only three.*

## Missile tank

The T-90 is the latest of Russia's main tanks. It has a 125-mm gun, which is bigger than most other tank guns today. This lets it fire a guided **missile** out of the tank's main gun. Using the missile, the T-90 can even attack helicopters!

## Britain's Challenger

The Challenger 2 tank has an unusual gun. It has grooves on the inside of the barrel. These make **shells** spin as they fly through the air. This makes them more accurate. The barrels of most tank guns are smooth inside. They do not make shells spin.

*Computers keep the Challenger 2's gun pointing at its target. This means the gun can fire accurately even when the tank is racing over rough ground.*

# The smartest tank design

The Israeli Merkava tank is different from most other tanks. It has a very clever design.

### Engine at the front

Tanks usually have their engine at the back. The Merkava is the only big battle tank that has its engine at the front. This gives the crew extra protection, like an extra layer of armour.

The Merkava's turret has a very sloping shape to deflect shells that hit it.

## Merkava Mark 4

| | |
|---|---|
| Crew: | **4** |
| Weight: | **65,000 kg/143,300 lb** |
| Top speed: | **60 kph/37 mph** |
| Armament: | **120-mm main gun, 3 machine-guns and a 60-mm mortar** |

The Merkava has a door, called a hatch, in the back.

hatch

## Safety first

Tank crews get in and out of their tanks through small doors in the top of the **turret**. But it is very dangerous to climb on top of a tank when the enemy might shoot at it. The Merkava has a door at the back. This means that its crew can get in and out whilst sheltering behind the tank.

## Carrying troops

The Merkava can also fit eight soldiers inside. It is the only tank in the world that can do this. It doesn't normally carry extra troops, but in an emergency it could rescue the crew of another tank.

The Merkava carries 50 rounds of ammunition for its main gun – more than most other tanks.

# The fastest tank

The British Scorpion tank holds the world record speed for a modern tank – 82.2 kph (51.1 mph). The Scorpion is a light tank. It is smaller than main battle tanks like the American Abrams. The crew is protected by light armour made from aluminium. Scorpions can be powered by a Jaguar sports car engine or a bigger diesel engine.

**Scorpion light tank**

| | |
|---|---|
| Crew: | **3** |
| Weight: | **8,075 kg/17,800 lb** |
| Top speed: | **82.2 kph/51.1 mph** |
| Armament: | **76-mm main gun and one machine-gun** |

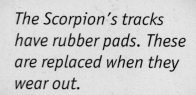

*The Scorpion's tracks have rubber pads. These are replaced when they wear out.*

S2000 PEACEKEEPER

Repaircraft PLC
S2000 PEACEKEEPER

## Speedy Peacekeeper

The tank that set the speed record is a version of the Scorpion called the S2000 Peacekeeper. It has a diesel engine. It set the record on 26 March 2002. Speed records are usually set on race-tracks, but tank tracks would damage a normal race-track. This record was set on a special test track in England. If the track had been longer, the tank could have gone even faster!

## SPEED MACHINES

◎ In the 1930s, the American T3 Christie tank reached the amazing speed of 112 kph (70 mph).

◎ The biggest battle tanks are much heavier than the Scorpion and so they are slower. The Leopard 2 is one of the fastest, at 72 kph (45 mph).

*This version of the American T3 Christie tank from the 1930s is unusual. It doesn't have a turret!*

# The strangest tank

Tank designers try to make tanks low so that enemies have a small target to shoot at. The Swedish Stridsvagn Strv-103 was made low and flat by having no turret. The gun is fixed on the tank's flat top. It cannot turn or tilt at all!

## Stridsvagn Strv-103

| | |
|---|---|
| Crew: | **3** |
| Weight: | **42,500 kg/ 93,710 lb** |
| Top speed: | **50 kph/30 mph** |
| Armament: | **105-mm main gun and machine-gun** |

## Turn and tilt

A tank's turret turns so that the gun can point in any direction. The gun can also be tilted up or down, so that the shell flies the right distance to the target. The Strv-103 has to have a way of doing the same thing with a gun that doesn't turn or tilt.

If the gun cannot move, then the whole tank has to move to take aim. First, the tank turns to point the gun in the right direction. Then, the whole tank tilts up or down. But this way of aiming causes problems. Most tanks can aim and fire while they are moving. The Strv-103 has to stop first. And when the tank tilts up, the enemy has a bigger target to fire at. So, no more tanks like the Strv-103 have been built.

*For a Strv-103 to take aim, the whole tank has to turn and tilt to fire the gun.*

# The heaviest tank

During World War II (1939–1945), some tank designers tried to build unbeatable tanks. They made tanks that had a huge gun with very thick armour. That made the tanks very big and heavy. These super-tanks were so heavy that they were far too slow.

## Mighty Maus

In 1943, Germany produced a tank called the Maus, meaning Mouse! It weighed an amazing 188 tonnes (more than 400,000 pounds). That's more than twice the weight of the heaviest tank today, the American M1A2 Abrams. It was so slow that you could pedal a bicycle faster! The Maus had a 128-mm (5-inch) main gun – far bigger than other tank guns of that time.

Germany's Maus tank was built in 1943. In this photo, the gun is hidden behind the turret.

## The armoured tortoise

The heaviest British tank was the A39 Tortoise. It was built in the 1940s, like the German Maus. The Tortoise was so heavy that no tank transporter of the day could carry it. In fact, it could hardly move by itself either! The Tortoise was cancelled soon after testing.

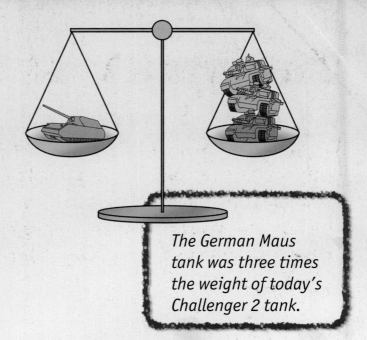

*The German Maus tank was three times the weight of today's Challenger 2 tank.*

*The Tortoise tank had the biggest gun of any British tank in the 1940s. The Tortoise was a failure because it was so heavy and slow.*

| | **Maus**  | **A39 Tortoise** |
|---|---|---|
| Crew: | 6 | 7 |
| Weight: | 188,000 kg/414,470 lb | 79,252 kg/174,720 lb |
| Speed: | 20 kph/12 mph | 20 kph/12 mph |
| Armament: | 128-mm main gun plus 75-mm gun and a 20-mm cannon | 94-mm main gun and 3 machine-guns |

# The greatest tank of its day

The Soviet T-34 tank fought in World War II (1939–1945). It was very advanced for the 1940s. It was fast, even on rough ground. It had thick armour. And it was equal in firepower to any other tank. The Soviet Union's enemy, Germany, had to build better tanks to match it.

## Sloping armour

The T-34 had sloping sides. These made it harder to destroy the tank. When shells hit its sloping armour, some of them just bounced off. And when the T-34 was damaged, it was quick and easy to repair.

The T-34 tank was better than the enemy tanks it faced in 1941.

## Keeping up with the enemy

At first, the T-34 was armed with a 76-millimetre (3-inch) gun. Soon, new German tanks like the Panther could match it, so a better T-34 was built. It had a bigger 85-millimetre (3.3-inch) gun. The new tank was called the T-34/85.

The German Panther tank was built to match Russia's T-34.

| | T34/76 | T-34/85 | Panther |
|---|---|---|---|
| Crew: | 4 | 5 | 5 |
| Weight: | 26,800 kg/59,085 lb | 32,000 kg/70,550 lb | 44,800 kg/98,767 lb |
| Speed: | 55 kph/34 mph | 55 kph/34 mph | 46 kph/29 mph |
| Armament: | 76-mm main gun and 1 machine-gun | 85-mm main gun and 2 machine-guns | 75-mm main gun and 2 machine-guns |

# The most numerous tank

About 50,000 T-72 tanks have been built since 1972. Nearly 30 armies around the world have used it. Over that long time, it has had new guns, more powerful engines, thicker armour, and the latest electronics.

## Cutting the crew

The T-72 needs a crew of only three soldiers instead of the usual four. Most tanks have a loader, whose job is to load the gun. The T-72's main gun loads itself, so the loader is not needed.

The T-72 tank has been built in great numbers.

## Exploding armour!

In the 1980s, the T-72 got a new type of armour. It is called **Explosive** Reactive Armour (ERA), because it is designed to explode! Exploding armour might seem like a crazy idea, but there is a good reason for using it. One type of **ammunition** used against tanks sends a jet of hot metal through the tank's armour. Exploding armour stops the jet from cutting through the tank.

### T-72

| | |
|---|---|
| Crew: | 3 |
| Weight: | 44,500 kg/98,105 lb |
| Speed: | 60 kph/37 mph |
| Armament: | 125-mm main gun and 2 machine-guns |

*Some T-72 tanks were fitted with Explosive Reactive Armour (ERA). It looks like thick flat tiles bolted onto the top of the tank.*

# Other popular tanks

The US M60 Patton tank was America's main battle tank for 20 years before the Abrams tank replaced it. It was used by the armies of 22 countries.

## Missile tank

The M60 was updated three times to make it better. The first update was called the M60A1. It had a new slimmer turret and thicker armour. The next update was the M60A2. It had a much bigger gun that could fire missiles as well as normal ammunition. The M60A2 didn't work very well. The missile system made it too complicated.

*The M60 tank was a very successful design. More than 15,000 M60 tanks were built*

## Third time lucky

The final update was the M60A3. It was the best and most successful. The missile system was taken out. The latest computer for aiming the main gun was installed. The M60A3 could be driven over obstacles nearly a metre (3 feet) high. It could cross gaps 2.6 metres (8 feet 6 inches) wide.

*The Israeli Sabra tank was developed from the M60.*

|  | **M60A3** | **Sabra** |
| --- | --- | --- |
| Crew: | 4 | 4 |
| Weight: | 51,700 kg/114,000 lb | 55,880 kg/123,200 lb |
| Speed: | 48 kph/30 mph | 48 kph/30 mph |
| Armament: | 105-mm main gun and 2 machine-guns | 120-mm main gun and 3 machine-guns |

# Tanks in action

Tanks have to fight on all sorts of ground. They can go fastest on roads, but they are more likely to be travelling across the countryside. They may have to cross soft ground or desert sand, or climb steep slopes. They may also have to go through water.

## Crossing water

Most tanks can go through water a metre or two (3–6 feet) deep. Some tanks can go through deeper water by using snorkels. A snorkels is a long pipe that fits on top of a tank so that air can get in. The engine needs a snorkel too, to let air in and waste gas out. The Russian T-80 tank can go through water 5 metres (16 feet) deep by using snorkels.

*Snorkels are used when tanks need to travel through very deep water.*

## Rescue tanks

Tanks sometimes break down and have to be rescued. Another tank makes the best recovery vehicle. A rescue tank doesn't need a gun. Instead, the **hull** has a crane on top. Other vehicles based on tanks include armoured bulldozers, bridge-laying tanks, and tanks that clear mine-fields.

*A bridge-laying tank can put down a folding metal bridge over a river in just a few minutes.*

# Facts and figures

There are dozens of tanks. Some of them are listed here. You can use the information to see which tanks are the biggest and heaviest, which have the biggest guns, and which are the fastest. Can you see how tank guns have got bigger over the years?

If you want to know more about these or other tanks, look on pages 30 and 31 to find out how to do some research.

## World War I tanks (1914–1918)

| Tank | Total length | Weight | Top speed | Main gun |
| --- | --- | --- | --- | --- |
| A7V Battle Tank (Germany) | 7.3 m/24 ft 1 in | 29,900 kg/65,920 lb | 8 kph/5 mph | 57-mm |
| Mark 1 (UK) | 9.9 m/32 ft 6 in | 28,450 kg/62,720 lb | 6 kph/4 mph | Two 6-pounders |

## World War II tanks (1939–1945)

| Tank | Total length | Weight | Top speed | Main gun |
| --- | --- | --- | --- | --- |
| A22 Churchill I (UK) | 7.4 m/24 ft 5 in | 39,575 kg/87,360 lb | 25 kph/15 mph | 2-pounder |
| A27 Cromwell (UK) | 6.4 m/20 ft 10 in | 27,940 kg/61,600 lb | 64 kph/40 mph | 6-pounder |
| A39 Tortoise (UK) | 10.1 m/33 ft 2 in | 79,252 kg/174,720 lb | 20 kph/12 mph | 32-pounder |
| M3 Grant (USA) | 5.6 m/18 ft 6 in | 27,215 kg/60,000 lb | 42 kph/26 mph | 75-mm |
| KV-1 (Russia) | 6.3 m/20 ft 7 in | 47,500 kg/104,720 lb | 35 kph/22 mph | 76-mm |
| M4 Sherman (USA) | 6.3 m/20 ft 7 in | 31,555 kg/69,565 lb | 42 kph/26 mph | 75-mm or 17-pounder |
| Maus (Germany) | 10.1 m/33 ft 2 in | 188,000 kg/414,470 lb | 20 kph/12 mph | 128-mm |
| PzKpfw V Panther (Germany) | 6.7 m/22 ft 6 in | 44,800 kg/98,765 lb | 46 kph/29 mph | 75-mm |
| PzKpfw VI Tiger I (Germany) | 8.3 m/27 ft | 55,000 kg/121,255 lb | 38 kph/24 mph | 88-mm |
| PzKpfw VI Tiger II (Germany) | 10.3 m/33 ft 9 in | 69,400 kg/153,000 lb | 38 kph/24 mph | 88-mm |
| T-34/85 (Soviet Union) | 8.2 m/26 ft 11 in | 32,000 kg/70,550 lb | 55 kph/34 mph | 85-mm |

## Modern tanks

| Tank | Total length | Weight | Top speed | Main gun |
|---|---|---|---|---|
| Ariete (Italy) | 9.7 m/31 ft 9 in | 54,000 kg/119,050 lb | 65 kph/40 mph | 120-mm |
| Challenger 2 (UK) | 11.5 m/37 ft 9 in | 62,500 kg/137,790 lb | 60 kph/37 mph | 120-mm |
| K1/A1 (Korea) | 9.7 m/31 ft 10 in | 54,500 kg/120,150 lb | 65 kph/40 mph | 120-mm |
| Leclerc (France) | 9.9 m/32 ft 6 in | 56,000 kg/123,459 lb | 70 kph/43 mph | 120-mm |
| Leopard 2 (Germany) | 9.7 m/31 ft 9 in | 62,000 kg/136,685 lb | 72 kph/45 mph | 120-mm |
| M1A2 Abrams (USA) | 9.8 m/32 ft 3 in | 70,655 kg/155,770 lb | 68 kph/42 mph | 120-mm |
| M60A3 (USA) | 9.4 m/30 ft 10 in | 51,700 kg/114,000 lb | 48 kph/30 mph | 105-mm |
| Merkava Mark 4 (Israel) | 9.0 m/29 ft 7 in | 65,000 kg/143,300 lb | 60 kph/37 mph | 120-mm |
| Olifant (South Africa) | 10.2 m/33 ft 6 in | 58,000 kg/127,870 lb | 60 kph/37 mph | 105-mm |
| Sabra (Israel) | 9.4 m/30 ft 10 in | 55,880 kg/123,200 lb | 48 kph/30 mph | 120-mm |
| Scorpion light tank (UK) | 4.8 m/15 ft 8 in | 8,075 kg/17,800 lb | 80 kph/50 mph | 76-mm |
| Stridsvagn Strv-103 (Sweden) | 9.0 m/29 ft 6 in | 42,500 kg/93,710 lb | 50 kph/30 mph | 105-mm |
| T-72 (Russia) | 9.5 m/31 ft 3 in | 44,500 kg/98,105 lb | 60 kph/37 mph | 125-mm |
| T-80 (Russia) | 9.7 m/31 ft 8 in | 46,000 kg/101,415 lb | 70 kph/43 mph | 125-mm |
| T-90 (Russia) | 9.5 m/31 ft 3 in | 46,500 kg/102,515 lb | 60 kph/37 mph | 125-mm |
| Type 90 (Japan) | 9.8 m/32 ft | 50,000 kg/110,000 lb | 70 kph/43 mph | 120-mm |
| Type 90-II (China) | 10.1 m/33 ft | 48,000 kg/105,820 lb | 65 kph/40 mph | 125-mm |

## Armour

Tank armour has to be tough enough to protect tank crews. At first, thick metal armour was used. When tanks were fitted with bigger guns, the armour was made thicker. But armour is very heavy. So designers looked for new ways of protecting tanks without using thicker metal. Modern tank armour is top secret. Some is made from a "sandwich" of metal and plastic. Armour made from different materials like this is called composite armour.

## Future tanks

Tanks could be made a lot smaller, and harder to attack, if they didn't have people inside them. So, future tanks may have no crews inside! The driver could sit in a control room, looking at a video screen. When the driver moves his controls, radio signals would make the tank move.

# Glossary

**ammunition** bullets or shells that can be fired from a gun

**armour** thick metal used to protect a tank crew from attack

**barrel** the long, tube-shaped part of a tank's gun, which shells are fired through

**commander** crew-member in charge of a tank. The commander decides where the tank should go and what it should shoot at.

**diesel engine** type of engine used by most tanks. Diesel engines are named after their inventor, Rudolf Diesel.

**explosive** substance that bursts out with a great force and noise. The shells fired by tanks are filled with explosives.

**gas turbine engine** type of engine used by the American Abrams tank. Fuel burned inside the engine heats air. Air expands as it heats up. The force of the air spins a turbine, like wind blowing a windmill but much faster. The spinning turbine drives the tank's tracks.

**gunner** member of a tank's crew who aims and fires the gun

**hull** main body of a tank

**loader** member of a tank's crew who loads the main gun. He also takes out the empty shell cases after the gun has been fired.

**machine-gun** type of gun that fires very quickly

**main battle tank (MBT)** a country's most important type of tank. MBTs form most of a country's tank force.

**main gun** the biggest gun a tank has

**missile** weapon that is powered by a rocket. It flies towards its target and explodes.

**mortar** short wide tube used to fire shells high in the air, to drop on nearby targets

**shell** metal case shaped like a bullet, which is full of explosives. It is fired from a large gun and explodes when it hits something.

**track** continuous metal belt, like a flattened bicycle chain, that goes around a tank's wheels. Tracks spread a tank's great weight over the ground so that it doesn't sink. The track links grip the ground better than a tyre.

**turret** top part of a tank where the main gun is. The turret turns round so that the gun can point in any direction.

# Finding out more

You can find out more by looking for other books to read and searching the internet.

## Books

Here are some more books about tanks:

*Designed for Success – Military Vehicles*, by Ian Graham (Heinemann Library, 2004)

*The Mega Book of Tanks*, by Lynne Gibbs (Chrysalis Children's Books, 2003)

## Tanks online

These web sites give more information about tanks:

*http://fas.org* – information from the Federation of American Scientists. Click on "US Weapons Systems" and then "US Land Warfare Systems" and pick a tank from the list of tracked vehicles.

*http://www.tankmuseum.org* – the web site of the Tank Museum in Bovington, in the United Kingdom.

*http://www.armytankmuseum.com.au* – the web site of the Royal Australian Armoured Corps Tank Museum.

## More to do

Can you find out what the Russian T-40 Light Tank had that tanks today don't have? (Answer on page 32.)

## The first tanks

Do you know how the first tanks were invented and where? You can find out about this at:

◎ *http://www.spartacus.schoolnet.co.uk/ FWWtankdevelop.htm*

You can find out more about historic tanks at:

◎ *http://www.tiger-tank.com* – a web site about the famous German Tiger tanks of World War II.

◎ *http://www.D-DayTanks.org.uk* – a web site about the tanks that landed in France on D-Day, 6 June 1944, to begin the liberation of Europe.

You can also find information about record-breaking tanks at *http://guinnessworldrecords.com*.

# Index

## Answer to question on page 30

A propeller! The Russian T-40 tank was an amphibious tank. This means it was designed to go through deep water as well as on land. It was shaped like a boat and so it had a propeller!